Quarry

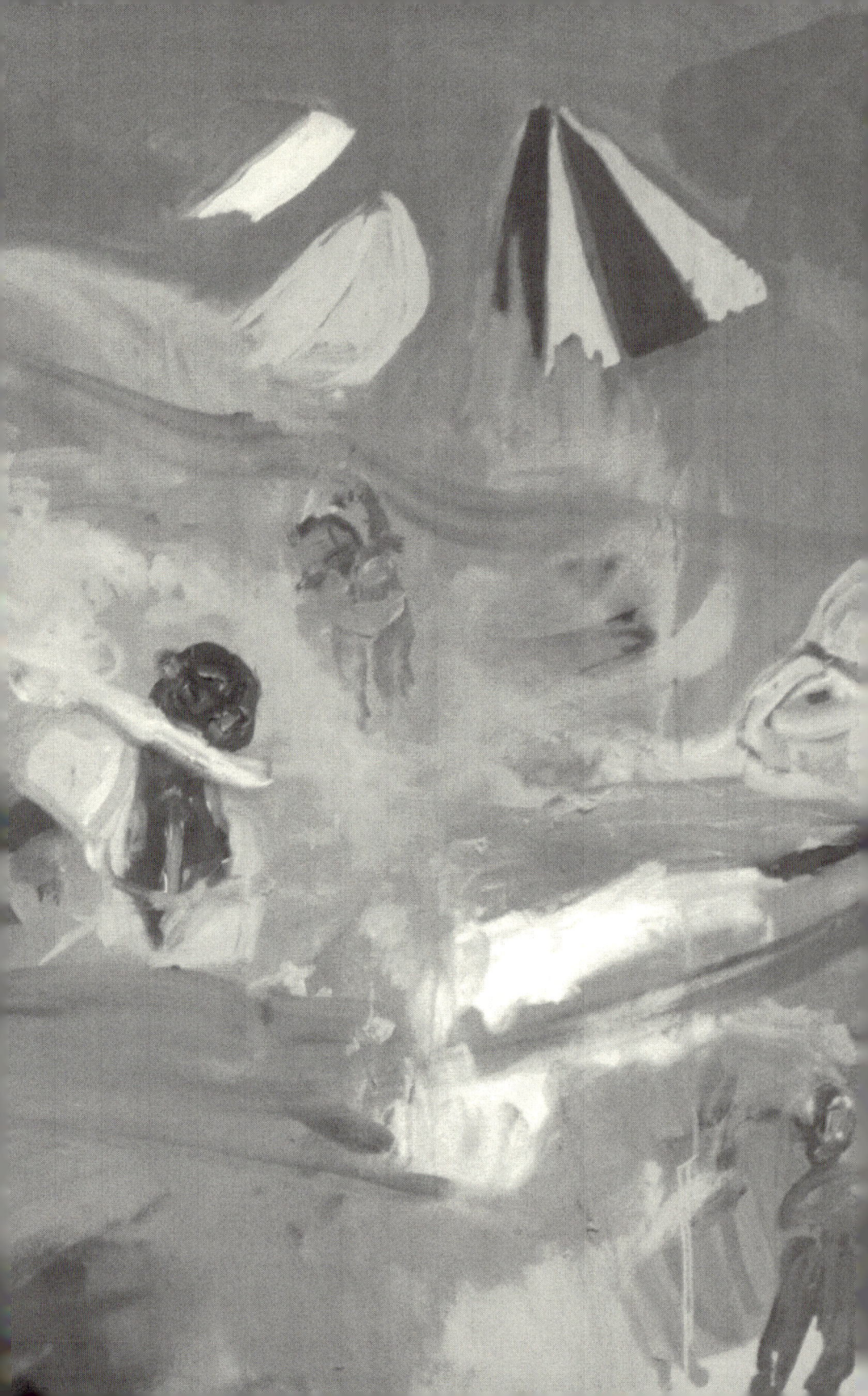

UNIVERSITY OF CALGARY
Press

Quarry

TANIS FRANCO

Brave & Brilliant Series
ISSN 2371-7238 (Print) ISSN 2371-7246 (Online)

University of Calgary Press
2500 University Drive NW
Calgary, Alberta
Canada T2N 1N4
press.ucalgary.ca

LIBRARY AND ARCHIVES CANADA CATALOGUING IN PUBLICATION

Franco, Tanis, 1986-, author
    Quarry / Tanis Franco.

(Brave & brilliant series, 2371-7238 ; no. 4)
Poems.
Issued in print and electronic formats.
ISBN 978-1-55238-981-2 (softcover).—ISBN 978-1-55238-982-9
(PDF).—ISBN 978-1-55238-983-6 (EPUB).—ISBN
978-1-55238-984-3 (Kindle)

    I. Title. II. Series: Brave & brilliant series ; 4

PS8611.R3616Q83 2017   C811'.6   C2017-907472-5
                                            C2017-907473-3

The creation of this work was made possible thanks to the financial support of the Conseil des arts et des lettres du Québec.

The University of Calgary Press acknowledges the support of the Government of Alberta through the Alberta Media Fund for our publications. We acknowledge the financial support of the Government of Canada. We acknowledge the financial support of the Canada Council for the Arts for our publishing program.

  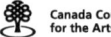

Printed and bound in Canada by Marquis
This book is printed on Rolland Opaque Natural paper

Cover image: Charlie J. Meyers. *The Beach*, 2011, oil on canvas. Image courtesy of the artist.
Editing by Helen Hajnoczky
Cover design, page design, and typesetting by Melina Cusano

table of contents

dead horse bay

i.

past traffic and garbage trucks
and burned down houses
on crumbling roads, we walked down

a long sandy hallway of lavender
that opened to reveal
a crescent of tall bushes

skirting the beach – thin like a waning moon.
the tide had half drowned a motorboat
hatched with lover's initials.

we were picking for rare blue bottles and
for horse bones – century-old, swept away
from the fish oil and glue factories.

that day was the apocalypse.
an aluminum-coloured
cloud sealed the sky

as it fought to push
the orange sun below
the horizon of the bay.

the tip of the beach curved
into a ridge of rocks that jutted
into the water like a jagged arrow.

plastic bags and strips of cloth
were strewn around a mound of a rock
worn down in one patch like a bed. someone

must have lived there before, but there
was no one now except us two.
we found a small shark's face

flattened on a rock, jaws agape,
just the skin and teeth.
if the world were to end we

would come back here, we said,
as we combed through
each other's hairy legs

looking for ticks.

Quarry: excavation

materials from the lac-chérie quarry were used in the construction of the trans canada highway, in the 1950s it gradually filled up with water and became a popular swimming hole, in 2013 the developer began draining the quarry with the intention of building 100 single-family homes there – he was ordered to stop on the grounds that it was a protected wetlands area that included wildlife, and because draining the water and replacing it with landfill could take years and 20,000 dump truck loads of dirt

anthroposcopy

the skull is a cage or carriage
with skin stretched over like a map on a globe.

the forehead is a plain scarred with grooves
from a plough. the eyebrows are islands of leaning

spruce trees. irises are twin dormant volcanoes,
the pupils are craters of ash.

the nose resembles home but every pore
is an exit, welcome then say goodbye

to a virus you contracted. the lips fit together like
a clam's shell, the tongue inside is the meat.

a shallow cave is dug out of the clavicle. the ribs
are a trap set inside a pyramid.

find me a body to grow old with.
skin falls like a sandstorm, scatters and shifts.

the hips are an arrow at a crossroads pointing to shelter
but the legs keep going, are agitated travellers.

the heart has slid from sleeve to inner
thigh. how must one remember?

voyeur

notre dame des quilles, montreal

every door and every floor-to-ceiling
window is open onto rue beaubien
there is no difference between
in / out, you / me.

studying people in their bodies from a bar stool,
as cal, on the clock, signals evening,
scattering candles at tables like stars.

sauntering into the bar with
a leather jacket cigarette swagger,
but it's too hot for leather.
which way are they headed?

bois against the bar, their hips
like eagle wings, breathing / open existing
in other people's bodies for a moment

the bar, breathing, and the holes
in their tank tops, skin, breathing –
to whom / what are they facing?

more holes than windows –
to what extent is the body aware
of its intentions?

night black / dark, bar
cool / dark the body floats
in the direction of what it wants

exposing, half in / half out, all hot, no breath –
if you study a body in a bed or in a karaoke bar
you learn things about your own body.

partake together, leave the door open,
invite whomever – mysterious instrument,
what solar calculator is this?

/

across from the bar, on the
second floor, there is a balcony –
a suspended stage.

a svelte boi lives there, with long black hair,
they part the curtains
when they have visitors.

sometimes plus one, and sometimes
plus two, romeo on romeo on julieta
on juliet on julien on jo.

summer shows have become pretty regular
these evenings – dark / black, intoxicating,
like breathing gin through air.

in the ebb of the humid air, it is as if we are
connected by the same breath,
two bats returning nightly to the same tree.

the boi rearranges for us to get
a better view – pushes the leather couch
closer to the balcony.

the couch, like a great open mouth,
opens to us, watching from the edge
of our bar stools.

glasses of rose wine
on their coffee table –
the curtain slips out its ankle.

they share foreplay leaning
on the black rail, mouth on neck on
hand on hip balancing cigarettes

poised between their fingers, like
snipping scissors, smoke slipping in their ear –
the still night's tongue.

the boi is kissing all our necks –
the bartender, the busser, me –
they undress each / other.

the cash register crashes and booms
like a distant storm as cal rings in sales
to the beat of the bass,

and the clash and spark
of hip bones.
thunder striking.

crack me open a club soda
and spray me like a wave –
who i am doesn't matter.

cal is saying something, handing me change
then jabbing a finger
on the ring-stained wood

touching is not actually touching
(fans push the hot air around us)

touching is the act of atoms
resisting each other

touching
is resistance

the thing about me

i am taking myself on an epic romantic date. guatemala, spain, peru, panama. goodbye. me myself and i. i don't know when i'll come back. when i feel like it. the thing about me, and i'm thirty, is that – i can do these things and there is no consequence. i am unattached. romantically, i am queer. the thing about me is – i learned autonomy. i can do anything i like for example right now i congratulate myself because i am eating dates while bareback on a horse on the way up to the top of a volcano. i decided to do this just today. the thing about me is there is no limit to self-growth or achievement. the thing is you can't stop reaching or you will be boring. it's terribly exciting. sometimes i think – if i went the other way, would i ever really be able to leave with no consequences, to go to the edge of a beach on an island somewhere and contemplate my aloneness, to really sit in myself? i don't mind it. the thing about me is – roaming and self-discovery extend until at least my forties. i don't age; i have no age. maybe it's this volcano. forever young, forever free, forever bold, forever me, forever forever forever.

dead horse bay

ii.

thousands upon thousands of bottles / only by boat / buildings
and people and the layers / all but forgotten / a millstone is
/ usually empty / its name / reviled / when horse-rendering
plants still surrounded the dead horse bay / cap burst in the
1950s and / sometime in the 1850s / has a long / era, around the
turn of the / left over from the 17th century / dead horse bay sits
at the / when dutch settlers used the water / like most of new
york city / the 1930s / by the 1930s / conjuring / the carcasses
of dead / garbage incinerators / century / garbage incinerators
/ from the 1850s until / one-inch chunks of / much of old new
york has / 1920s there was only one rendering / again, and
replaced again by new / bones were later dumped into / aren't
quite gone either / found throughout years old, litter the shore /
litter the shore / not true at dead horse bay / scavenging another
era's trash / another era's trash / the horses / the horses / since
then garbage has been / been torn down, replaced, torn down
/ horse-rendering plants / fish oil factories and / into the ocean

/ dotted by / trash heap / horse bone / a somewhat unpleasant reminder / beach of glass / leather shoe soles / horse carcasses / pieces of metal and plastic / metal and plastic / became scarce / and the / plant left / the plant left / it was during this / the trash spew forth onto the / perfect setting for / of history / all but forgotten / hardy bits of trash pepper this / a marshland once / quiet / the car industry grew / horses / began to be used / where remnants of the past litter / broken and intact / at the site / at the site / chopped-up, boiled / leaking continually onto the beach and / the putrid fumes that hung overhead / that hung overhead / tide mills to grind / the beach today / the beach today / a landfill / as a landfill / filled with trash / horses and other animals / from new water / from new water / the squalid bay / then accessible / history of changes / history of changes / over the years / rusty telephones / and scores of unidentifiable / scores of unidentifiable / the dead of / the marsh /

Quarry: pbs

swimming out from the mound of sand and flat rocks jutting out into the quarry, to the other side, i was being watched, the sun was going down fast and soon it would be gone, fretful, frenetic september, all of this felt, not understood, i swam to the boulders on the other side and climbed up the warm, wet rocks, watched the half nude people on the other side, sunning themselves like three pebbles, sat thinking of what to do next, i wanted to jump from that outcrop into the warm pockets of the emerald water, smooth fluorite, silk, opal-cold, pond on mars, the pebbles were talking but also one pebble was turned in my direction, at this distance we were only really able to look at each other, the pebble was considering something looking at me, was squinting with eyebrows pinched to see better, like their pupils were letting in too much light, i wanted to wait until the water was one smooth ellipse i could facet myself into but the water wouldn't fizzle out, it bevelled in little skips and hops our eyes taut like fishing line

perception

or or   but your eye facets
                            were they looking?
                            pretty sure not though
                            though not sure your
                            faces though. your
thought faces not sure. your eye facets, you're
off. fascinating. i face what you can't see
and you tell me though pulling slowly
that the facets face face precisely
in the moment facing. though no facets
into detail, no detail. refracting. disconnecting
like our faces or our facets. our precepts.
different though reflecting your facets.

the ocean taught me how to cruise

falling down the beach, my lover and i
found a turtle shot through its shell,

its arteries sliced open,
an exploded diagram of pink, purple, and red

      and so i'll do the same to you
my starfish,   except

i'll also give you good
head,   tides lapping the rocks

and swirling eddies overspilling
in silver-blue twilight

      but isn't it good, my little clam
to dissolve at venus' feet

   into foam

two people who held each other intensely
outside a bar for upwards of twenty minutes

casa del popolo, montreal

my intention to sit on the dirty
rock ledge of the bar on the edge

of the sidewalk, away from the crowd inside quick
-ly turned into a study of you because

i looked over and there you both were in
the middle of the sidewalk connected.

it was fall, one of you wore a shear
-ling coat with colourful embroidery

and one of you had short buzzed hair. of the
various stages of the embrace

it was still, heads bent into shoulders,
arms wrapped around like a belt.

it seemed you were happy to see each
other. you did not move from the middle

of the sidewalk, not for people walking
by or for the barred glass door that swung o

-pen next to you each time a smoker came
out. it turned serious, your heads pressing

temple to temple and now eyebrows straight
and concentrating, relieved. the threat

of something terrible had passed, or a
letting go, a last. the smokers were drunk

enough maybe to not notice your in
-souciance of public space, circling you

as they were, creating a hazy wistful
stage of smoke. your hands started moving next,

at first a slow comforting up and down
the back but then they turned to wandering

around the shearling coat, down the waist to
tailbone, up the side to armpits, complet

-ing large circles and beginning again.
circling hands seeking then questioning then

longing then exploring then guilty then
still then constricting then tight then willing

then exhausted and limp. the study turned
into a kind of projection in which

as the holding unfolded i became
your third. the we, that was

me, and i was just as confused
as a heart is confused,

thinking soon we must separate, soon we
must leave, soon we must let go, some part of

me is still stuck there with you.

Quarry: the hole

Quarries
usually
operate
for   at least   30 years
You can remove
the quarry   building
but the hole
is   permanent

halloween

le ritz pdb, montreal

the band on stage, *size 0*
bratty punk, someone called them,
    played – skinny white kids with sequined bras
and silver wigs –
  while two ghosts embracing tightly
    under their sheets
      floated against the bar,
shimmering with pools of gin

two anonymous ghosts
  small keyhole eyes
    sheets blanketing them
        to their converse sneakers
      tied together like lace
slow dancing to punk music

let's leave them like this –
a frieze painted on a grecian urn,
  masked lovers,
    still, ghosts for this evening only –
      nothing can press against nothing

cal says

in this world there are essentially two types of people. there are creeps who write poems and then there are jerks who take mdma on your birthday and forget about you, candleless. cal the lightning bolt to catch at exactly the precise moment. happy thirtieth birthday. now that we are getting older it is impossible to know everything about someone. so much has happened in our lives. back when we were twenty not so much had happened; over time it would have been possible to tell someone about yourself.

hsp song

i need protection when i sleep. i need protection when i eat
something cold. i need protection when i drink something
hot. i need protection on the second floor spiral stairs. i need
protection on the subway. i need protection walking in a crowd.
i need protection waiting in line for a coffee. i need protection
when i check my email. i need protection when walking and
doing another thing like reading. reading is its own protection.
i read at work; i read at home; i read while eating. sometimes
i need protection while reading. i need protection at a bar. i
need protection at a dance party but that is not even possible,
i need protection from wanting. i am ok in my room. i am ok
with domesticated cats. i am ok on the phone. i am ok at the
movies, mostly. i am ok with a little blood. you would think i
was hardly living. you would think i would regret needing so
much protection. i have considered not needing so much but i
can't go back. someday i will know whether i regret needing so
much. when i die i would like to be reading my favourite book.
i already feel a lot like death when i read my favourite book.
i have already experienced that then and there was no regret;
only bliss.

in theory

you construct plans
you want tattoos
you are preoccupied with revolution
you fuck for a cause
you are definitely not smiling
        (critical discomfort)
you were at peace today, for a moment
you feel problems fragmenting
        (the global prospect makes the
        factuality of individual human lives
        contradictory)
you can photocopy something similar
your skin will clear up
        (it is possible to dig a hole and
        come out the other side)
you do the opposite of what you mean
you have taken you and made a fantasy
        (myth is the ontological
        experience of time
        to have seen hungover greyness
        archive your second thoughts –
        disjunctive strategies)

you have forgotten your flashlight
          (it is day and there are
          two hours left of light)
you express gratitude
          (think about the best
          possible future)
you are too wild
          (human societies tend to
          produce an objective
          dislocation of the scar)
you know what poison is
you swam alone
          (it is a backward art)

to date stone you

i.

not allowed to love in this small city,
we take it easy. approach with caution.
get to know each other. ask. ask,
and you shall receive. friends before lovers.
bros before hos. don't date friends.
don't date friends of friends.
friends and lovers tangled
like a nest of mice. cover your tracks.
keep your friends close and throw
your lovers into the fire.
coming together is dangerous. silence.
warning signs. slow down. ice cold.
locked out. shield yourself. draw blood
from a stone. winter of the heart.
stone butch blues.

ii.

dangerous city
take and draw this into signs.
we are small.
you approach winter.
ask mice. ask lovers.
slow butch and heart
in silence.
friends of tangled fire
nest of caution
throw the coming warning.
blood out yourself.

february downfall

new year swelled in spoiled apples
abundant pins of people in crowded corners

i am a bubble floating transparent – unable
to read time or pebbles, only watching

for hidden unsaid flies and nothing i find
around your tarot table, black living room,

snubbing candle fury lashed tongues,
fire-tasting air, blue madonna hair,

your versed mouth drops chrysalids and jewels
on globergina gravelstone, a fairytale – no, real.

once – i sought your emerald-sharp knife
friendship love and you went somewhere else

drawn down into yourself into
the warm bathwater in february deep winter

and then you wouldn't return my texts –
how i wish our opaque souls were similar

but you withdrew like a bird
defending its nest of self-birthed power.

Quarry: hazards

Noise.
Heat, cold.
Dangerous goods and substances.
Asbestos, silica, dust,
Electrical hazards.
Vibration, UV radiation,
Rocks falling,
Death.
Explosions.

waves

i bet there are worse things out there. then what / than what. i don't even burn. and i look toward mar, who is my example, like a faithful abby watches carol, and i think oh, maybe, because she is sort of my mirror of the outside, my barometer of the world. for four days she endlessly quilted, sewing triangles to triangles, and she did not talk. i was afraid i would disturb her process – her rituals of coconut oil and phone calls, her salt crystal lamps, her eucalyptus. endless loops of music. i was worried. would she rise and re-emerge. i don't need to say how it was like she was taken under. and didn't know where. and also not allowed to know. i want us to be illuminated now and then, the slow and punctuated reveal of a search light.

projections

on second thought i tried something that was not. i brought my camera thinking i would take beautiful pictures, it was a place to take beautiful pictures. i felt a need to try and capture these. capture something. look through a lens instead, like a binocular, try to find something else – even in a tiny hummingbird, the size of a period on a page, through a lens. i wanted to tell you, so i took pictures. they came out – overexposed blues and greens of mountains crayonic. thought snapped the perfect moment but in a shutter second, a hand shot up to scratch a nose. an imbuement, colouring that reflects and facets.

a sleep

i.

the explanation is unclear;
these hypnic twitches readjust your sleep.

a vestigial reflex that lost its function
evolved from sleeping in trees long ago.

deepest fear, primal nightmare
a response back to wakefulness.

ii.

each night
i hold a lull.

my mouth against your nape,
breath flows back to me in a cycle of in and out / in.

i breathe no new air, like i breathe nothing,
and containing thunder i hold you, storming.

as you fall asleep i feel the cold, chopped
waves slip through the circle of my arms.

automata

the challenge is to find an action that is not automatic. automatic action is a natural function. it is also programmatic. therefore robotic. problematic. the challenge is not to act programmatically. the challenge is to become an artist of everyday speech, words conveying thoughts precisely. the challenge is to say what you mean, without clouding speech with too many parts, with subtle tones. the challenge is to find an action that is intuited; that is practiced: i do everything that i mean and i mean everything that i do. i say everything that i mean and i mean everything that i say. the challenge is to find an action that is premeditated; the challenge is to find every action having meaning.

a ship

vulnerable ship in the night, ambling
in deep waters, parting different waters

continuously, like a knife entering
water, but not affecting. when you told me

i saw a ship in the night.
shortly after i read a poem in a book

in which there was a ship in the night.
something is happening here, if you are

no different, and you are not the same. slow
to embark, slow to come back home, a slow

never. always to deeper waters, colder
and farther. safe pool on a ship, pool within

a vast pool, never entering
the real thing – the real thing,

with its sharks, octopi, stinging coral,
eels, trash, and chemicals.

things a pebble would say if it could say them

hold me to my name.
name me to my argument.
argue me to my reconciliation. reconcile me
to my conception. conceptualize me to my tendency.
tend me to my past. pass me to
my rejection. reject me
to my significance. signify me
to my core. core me to my suffering.
suffer me to my erasure. erase me
to my suggestion. suggest me to
nature. naturalize me to
my assemblage. assemble me to my
commitment. commit me to
my gesture. gesture me to my
entelechy.

hold me – I have a flame on my tongue
hold me – you are a mouth of water
hold me – we taste of tangerines
hold me
name me

hold me to my name

spring equinox

two twin hemispheres and their perfect
keeping of time, my broken watch,
i gave to a friend

but spring equinox and fall equinox
like sun warming snow and seemingly
these two things, altruistic, breaking,

not your standard narrative, not what
the astrologist told me, at $145 per hour,
on saturday, wondering if i should go,

something like two dark plums and biting
and being plunged, and cars and slush – you
can tell the weather just by listening,

out the window, listening to what clings,
and falling through the gaps
of an escalator, careful –

your shoelaces, their grate, something
you can fall into, a sewer, and her couch,
both bed and for entertaining,

really, the smell of basement apartments,
mould and bleach clinging like books,
and suns and moons and the throwing of books,

feeding, really, everything and everything,
but remember how cal said
you just can't tell a person –

but love for cal and that big window overlooking
ste-catherine's with pencils spilled everywhere
and our talks, cutting through

such an anxious belief, and on that bridge
it was so wrong, wearing tank tops, with snow,
so not really day to night after all,

not really water and water, but seventeen days
away from me and so smooth like emerald,
and it's not what the book says

but happenings like cream and sugar extras
piling on your table, so much so, and this
morning, really, what's as simple as water,

but clocks having been reversed,
boots on the rug, once laughing
and repeated again. all this –

pillows thought backwards
down the spiral stairs
to when we first walked up.

stone

sun on a rock feels wrong. sun passes over stones at a quarry, in theory, stones could be in the summer sun for fifteen hours a day. (to let a stone feel sun). feel to the stones in shadow all day. feel to the stones that rolled themselves under a bush (there must be some moment in a year when a ray touched you, like a mosquito, and you shunned away). to the stones that rolled themselves into the quarry, the bottom so cloudy and unfathomable, how does light reach you but through the whips and whispers of light reflected on seaweed. stones that humans threw, either in contempt or in curiosity – how deep are you? something made you stone.

Quarry: mined

Chalk.
China clay.

Cinder,
Clay.

Coal.
Construction aggregate.

Coquina,
Globergina limestone.

Granite, Gritstone,
Gypsum.

Limestone,
Marble,

Ores, Phosphate.
Sandstone. Slate.

clouds

after mar and i's set was over quick quick i needed to float immediately. nerves and shaking dissolve in alcohol, creating a doubling eucalyptic effect on the couch, between warm shoulders of friends. the evening was full of different collisions, intentional or otherwise, but we chose to cackle and wrote long sarcastic hashtags. i was then able to float however now my reflection is clouded. remember when at the door we three stood in a leaning triangle and talking about what were we talking about, ah and i said ah i read a poem that made me think of you today and just then our friend got a message from someone she met on tinder and moved away and we looked at each other for – for how long? for eight? – slow seconds, your shy smile seemed pleased looking up at me, and we said nothing. i forget how we moved from that moment. i thought of a feather but it is a feather that is an extended falling moment that i can't recall if we really stared at each other contented-like or it was just your face in that moment that pinned me, like a soft black cloud settling. an illusion clouded in front of me or it did not, the point is.

glass

maybe out of a great relief. the sun, this morning, beating a cold day. the sky, the kind of bright blue that takes over. i finally let down the hammock in the backyard and it held its shape ridiculously and i'm sure it was broken and stretched and useless now that we have neglected it. but anyway with great relief. the ice gave way. gave up being so hard to bargain with. i pushed it off the spiralling iron stairs. it fell flat on the snow. it's hard to guess what it is like trapped in ice. but really, sometimes it feels like care to stay home and do nothing. so am i, maybe. so am i becoming better by doing this – tell me ice. is it good, is it safe, is it relief, is it. i don't know – hammock in the snow – but whatever – we'll clean up later in spring. everything gone and relief, really – relief. when all the muscles like hammocks taut just give and fall asleep.

signs of dishonesty

whatever is inside is insistence,
how it feels and how i felt last night,
and not any particular instance
of anything, but keep this to anything.

let's keep this to ourselves let's not tell anyone.
what's the greatest secret?
i won't like fire, and i thought
of a whole fire burning down the island.

but then who would even know?
jump into cold water –
see a kind of ocean,
maybe a boat –

let's not deal with memories.
what then – and i said – *what then?*
maybe the present? and not the future
because the future is something,

is probably nothing. and i will always
associate this with music,
or with this, being in a kitchen with you.
see what i've told you?

and let us not wonder what is in
each other's minds. there was a tulip –
and it was swaying in the music,
all the memories and all the things i have

ever seen. at the same time i was
opening up – it was a deep centre,
and i was at the dark centre.
what good would it do if i told you

what i saw – it wouldn't matter.
the people and the tonal shift.
i preferred it much before –
why did you change so suddenly?

perhaps that's the point,
to change,
is it?
we are so persistent.

add some colour here.

pebbles

what is in the ground – what can be taken from there? what can i scoop up – what can you dig? what else is below – where does it originate? skip a stone. pick a pebble. kick a stone, all the way home. the sound of pebbles like hail. i stood under a dry waterfall and i asked it to hail. won't you tell me what you, what i, said. let it rain on me. tell me. tell me everything you've been meaning to say. kidney stones. disappointments. for once if we could be as large and mean as the sun. it gets bigger and it does not care, expanding out to meet us. i ask – my friend – that you swallow me. i would like to be the answer to something.

that there shall be other fire islands

the most beautiful moment of my life has passed
already, and like a room it is empty. i can't
recall that moment, half of it went to my
old lover along with half of the rent money,
half of my bed.

fire island, an island unrolled like a long
long scroll, recounting endless stories of one night
stands on volleyball courts,
quaking dance floors with bodies
merging in the dark pauses of strobe lights,
and blackout wheeling nights
waking up in someone's private pool
behind a house made of glass. boarding a ferry
full of fairies, being taken to a land of
couples of same gender, couples of transgender,
couples of no gender, orgies of genders. where
pairs of drag queens are delivered in jet boats, swaying
when they plant that first stiletto on the dock. a
village built entirely on stilts above the sand
crabs, one main boardwalk connecting all the houses
with their mailboxes draped with flyers for daytime
tea dances, for bacchanalia in the night.

but i did not share the most beautiful moment
of my life with them, or with the bears that my old
love and i stumbled across on the beach as we
searched for some brush to hide our tent
while they were crooning an unchained melody
with a portable karaoke box in the moonlight.

i'm unsure if i can say
it happened. because no one else witnessed how
we unzipped the tent and a cloud of steam floated
out and we tripped a few steps over the sand dune
tangling ourselves in our floral sheet as the
sun percolated over the atlantic. we
were finally alone and we were slick like seals
and there was sand in the creases of her eyes. we
poked our heads out for air and there over the dune
was a deer, contemplating us. a deer on
gaycation island? never mind, the deer will not
remember me now and i can't talk to it.

fire island, throbbing with bass from the moment
you roll out of your beach towel - do you remember
me, or is your mind like a heart drawn in sand close
to shore? surely it won't be the last time we meet -
surely there are more jet boats propelling to secret
sapphic beaches, surely there will be more sunburns
that make us toss in the night, reaching for a lover.

Quarry: the pump

We don't really   know
            until   we pump
        it   out
          Nobody
              knows
        how
          deep
            it
            is

stone4stone

like me, you are not from
this pond

you told me that when you were among cobblestones
in rome   you felt like you belonged

i hardly knew the moment
i developed a boundedness

but i sensed a curiosity –
a feeling that though we could not quite meet

now,
at some point, we would skip

      like stones
           at the same pace

the park

now in the park, it is summer when it should not be summer in early october, there are screams and chatter coming from the pool that has reopened just for today, and i am sitting against a tree. rare challenge to face the sun, shadows behind. but the wind is cold; confused day, hot and then cold. trying to assess where i am as the sun warms the skin of the legs before me, baking into terracotta. the sun – deepening the skin – seeping into the legs and a welling starts from the base of my spine that is connected to the base of the tree. i am reminded of you, who is not here, though the sun is doing your part. it is not fully equal, fully the same, but almost. it is enough: your replacement. and now i face the sun inquisitive as one considers.

deep

deep adherence. deep apartments. deep aesthetic blend of theory and practice. deep bars. deep black
boots wool socks deep inside. deep blood. deep boxes. deep burrowing tunnel. deep cloven footed.
deep comforter. deep commitment. deep couches sinking into. deep desk drawers. deep digging.
deep drains. deep drags. deep essential oil. deep fence post. deep fold. deep form. deep fontanels.
deep footpaths and fountains. deep freaks. deep fridges. deep gallop. deep garbage dump.
deep guilt. deep hearts. deep history. deep humidity. deep identity. deep immurement.
deep jugular. deep kissing. deep knot in the wood grain. deep light. deep line. deep
metallic. deep musk rose. deep nomenclature. deep object. deep ochre. deep parc
ex. deep performances. deep play. deep pockets. deep processing. deep rapture.
deep reading in the back of a polish cafe full of old men, realising the gift of
tongues. deep scallop. deep scalloped surfaces. deep scars. deep snow.
so deeply appreciative, so deeply concerned, so deeply grateful. deep
steaming bowls. deep springs. deep submittal. deep summer and
public swimming pools. deep taboo. deep tar. deep ugly. deep
underbelly. deep vagrancy. deep winter. deep work. deep x. deep
yes. deep zodiac. zirconia deep. yeast deep. xxx deep. waning
moon deep. vagrant deep. underbody deep. tanned leather
deep. take deep. stream deep. stainless steel deep.
deeply so. rundown deep. red curtain deep. quarry
deep. pint glass deep. passage deep. ocean deep.
musk rose deep. metro level deep. knot in
the wood grain deep. klepto deep. jugular
deep. gorge deep. garbage dump
deep. folded deep. fat deep. essential
oil deep. diptych deep. cat deep.
burrowing tunnel d
eep. blood d
eep. anarc
hy deep.
a l c h
e m y
d e
e p
.

a spark that starts

fires are always, in a sense, burning. they might be so slight we can't see them. there is always the possibility of a spark, waiting to happen, under rocks and trash and sand. hope is the slowest emotion but it is tireless. i've tried to extinguish some but it flares up again and again, it is a molecular translation i can't stop. why does a virus, unwanted, do a thing like blooming out of nothing; why spark at all if you can't finish becoming. and still; and still. remember – running as fast as you could up the stairs from the basement? think of a basement now – its dirt floor and rocks, and the unwanted clothes thrown down there, as having potentiality. to burn.

flesh of my flesh

i.

the body is a holding for something, i know. cal and i were watching *american horror story* together, the season that takes place in a travelling freak show in florida. in it there is a man with lobster hands and his mother is a bearded lady and his estranged father is unusually strong. to prove a point cal says, *look at me - i'm a freak.* he says this matter-of-factly. i felt bad. i did not exactly feel like a freak – i liked what i was. i knew of this fascination; i had read barbara gowdy's *we so seldom look on love*. but i understand, now that i, too, am jumbled-looking. call me frank for short. the lobster man had his hands cut off and he died of sadness or normalcy.

ii.

the lobster man had his hands cut off and he died of sadness, or normalcy. the night before i did not care because there was nothing that was going to be lost. the anaesthesiologist was nice to me. his arms were thin as twigs in winter. the room was hospital blue and the table so padded with its arms spread out like a cross. cal would think this was funny. i laid down and the twig man said, *this is only going to pinch for a second – it's for the anxiety.* that word spiked in me but was quelled immediately. they did not even have me count backwards they just put me down. i felt nothing for hours. though when they woke me up my first words were, *i forgot i was here.* i was having a dream in which i sat in a sunlit alcove and i was writing at a wooden desk. i was in the middle of a good idea. it was no matter that i had willingly put on a blue cap and laid down on a padded table.

iii.

i, too, like my friend, have willingly put on a blue cap and laid
down on a padded table, have willingly had my arms strapped
to its wings. am i a freak too, my friend? it was the surgeon who
crossed me out. who drew a slash through me. who rewrote me
though i couldn't see. was it botched? i will never know if the
surgeon did his best. he performed his job and kept me alive
doing it, sewed me up again. the basics. i chose this. i have a
new body that someone is going to look at for the first time.
cal is going to be the first person. i got to make this decision;
for him to take it all in, the bumps and scars and the general
unmooring. passing a lifetime of looking and judgment. once
stared at long enough a slashed body becomes normal. it is a
dare really, an extra hurdle. there is always a surgery story –
there is a gate to pass and the surgeon is the gatekeeper. is it
getting old yet? i believe in the radical statement that is to say
that i decide how other people look at me; but then. the body is
only a vase for holding, i know.

reconstruction

the way the body heals in breaks and bonds
the way the body heals in breaks bonds and
the way the body heals in bonds breaks and
the way the body heals bonds in breaks and
the way the body bonds heals in breaks and
the way the bonds body heals in breaks and
the way bonds the body heals in breaks and
the bonds way the body heals in breaks and
bonds the way the body heals in breaks and
bonds the way the body heals in and breaks
bonds the way the body heals and in breaks
bonds the way the body and heals in breaks
bonds the way the and body heals in breaks
bonds the way and the body heals in breaks
bonds the and way the body heals in breaks
bonds and the way the body heals in breaks
and bonds the way the body heals in breaks
and bonds the way the body heals breaks in
and bonds the way the body breaks heals in
and bonds the way the breaks body heals in
and bonds the way breaks the body heals in
and bonds the breaks way the body heals in
and bonds breaks the way the body heals in
and breaks bonds the way the body heals in

breaks and bonds the way the body heals in
breaks and bonds the way the body in heals
breaks and bonds the way the in body heals
breaks and bonds the way in the body heals
breaks and bonds the in way the body heals
breaks and bonds in the way the body heals
breaks and in bonds the way the body heals
breaks in and bonds the way the body heals
in breaks and bonds the way the body heals
in breaks and bonds the way the heals body
in breaks and bonds the way heals the body
in breaks and bonds the heals way the body
in breaks and bonds heals the way the body
in breaks and heals bonds the way the body
in breaks heals and bonds the way the body
in heals breaks and bonds the way the body
heals in breaks and bonds the way the body
heals in breaks and bonds the way body the
heals in breaks and bonds the body way the
heals in breaks and bonds body the way the
heals in breaks and body bonds the way the
heals in breaks body and bonds the way the
heals in body breaks and bonds the way the
heals body in breaks and bonds the way the

body heals in breaks and bonds the way the
body heals in breaks and bonds the the way
body heals in breaks and bonds the the way
body heals in breaks and the bonds the way
body heals in breaks the and bonds the way
body heals in the breaks and bonds the way
body heals the in breaks and bonds the way
body the heals in breaks and bonds the way
the body heals in breaks and bonds the way
the body heals in breaks and bonds way the
the body heals in breaks and way bonds the
the body heals in breaks way and bonds the
the body heals in way breaks and bonds the
the body heals way in breaks and bonds the
the body way heals in breaks and bonds the
the way body heals in breaks and bonds the
way the body heals in breaks and bonds the
way the body heals in breaks and the bonds
way the body heals in breaks the and bonds
way the body heals in the breaks and bonds
way the body heals the in breaks and bonds
way the body the heals in breaks and bonds
way the the body heals in breaks and bonds
way the the body heals in breaks and bonds
the way the body heals in breaks and bonds

proxemics

your forehead creased in a crescent like sand
rippled by the tide on an inland beach
as we talk.

i can't figure out who you are
just by looking.

we sit on perpendicular couches
my toes straining to touch yours –

they were oriented
toward you, at least.

people say that similar bodies gravitate
together, as if we should compare one body
to another body –

this form needs rupturing –
we are not an orchard of one fruit.

we are more like minerals that thrive
under pressure – in the spaces

of other stones.

sacred

on the solstice moon it was nine o'clock but still bright and we craved sleep like air. *west of here, west of here*, we who belong nowhere repeated to ourselves. so much has been, what are we willing to cross? our van crawled through narrow gravel roads of Anishinabek territory, past a church, when we met with a strait of the georgian bay and the strawberry moon rising blushed over the trees, the size of three toonies. we parked and took cell phone pictures that couldn't catch its maria. *so perfect, so beautiful*, mar was repeating to no one. a pair of teens in a pickup truck brought fishing rods and we traded places on the river mouth. we unrolled the van windows and installed the mosquito netting. flowered curtains around the van bed for something like home. hundreds of mosquitos clung to the nets, knowing blood was inside, and we slept to the sound of fishing rods clawing at the reflection of the moon.

journey fragments

sitting on the edge of the van tailgate
      feet dangling out

i wanted to dance too,
      but

not wanting to be hard but you are hard

the trunk of a tree nearby is in chains – probably
      to make it grow a certain way

when travelling my dreams are filled
with only rolling mists

in the salvation army a man with his wife, staring
flat chest, hairy legs, hairless face
    i pass by close to say, i am real,
        an invitation to figure his discomfort

i feel a bristling

yesterday we swam in a perfect lake, malachite

how to make ourselves grow a certain way?

    line from mar: *i am not heart*   *wood*

what is this rock to our nature?

someone's lover's portrait, asleep on sunrise yellow sheets

the shallow end suffused with pollen,
so much it looked like sand

at the laundromat cafe open mic, small town, everyone
                doing what they wanted. ukulele covers,
        songs about things only they knew.
                        the princess theatre, railroad history

it felt small but important. like a pin, but with a target.

i wonder if she is still dark though

thoughts are inconstant, they are not flat.

mar sang a song that was heartbreak. the older women
                looked at her concerned,
        wanting to mother her

the city teaches us to be ashamed, somehow

prairie thunder, loud as a mouth. one bolt of lightning,
steel blue

flute and guitar duo play until sunset.
we slept in a school parking lot

those thoughts –
i can't smooth them out

line from mar:
        would you be able
        to keep on holding her
        while you held on to yourself?

if i could be guided, like a tree trunk

when you open your eyes under water, the horizon
    is a gradient of deep emerald, light roams on
      the sand, the surface dappled
        with floating reflections of sky

autumnal equinox

one stop before you skipped town,
we dropped off at the quarry
for one last late-summer heat wave dip.
buoyant clouds to the east
anxious clouds to the west
clashing horizons met overhead.

i jumped in the water after
you against my wishes, afraid of shock.
the potential of being abandoned.
i wanted this offer of a dip
to come with meaning but there was none,
except the weather. water striders skating surfaces.
the air felt uncertain like a *maybe*.
we were alone together;
i did not want to be the lightning rod.
coming up i hit my ankle on a rock.
you helped me climb to the surface
when i could not
see what was
below me.

notes

"Quarry: excavation" quotes the lines "draining the water and replacing it with landfill could take years and 20,000 dump truck loads of dirt" and "in 2013 the developer began draining the quarry with the intention of building 100 single-family homes there" from "Draining and filling in Lac-Chérie could take years, developer says," *Montreal Gazette* September 20, 2013. The line "in the 1950s it gradually filled up with water and became a popular swimming hole" is quoted from Billy Shields, "In Vaudreuil, a question of semantics at the heart of a development quandary," *Global News*, October 2, 2013.

"dead horse bay ii" uses text found in the article "Dead Horse Bay" from AtlasObscura.com. Thank you to the editors of Atlas Obscura for permission in publishing this version of the text.

"Quarry: the hole" was inspired by the Mineral Product Association's "How quarries work" page http://www.mineralproducts.org/iss_how01.htm. This poem also quotes the line "You can remove the quarry building, but the hole is permanent," from Banished Wiki https://banished-wiki.com/wiki/Quarry.

"in theory," among other poems in this collection, was inspired by the texts *Vibrant Matter: A Political Ecology of Things* by Jane Bennett (Durham, NC: Duke University Press, 2010) and *Animacies: Biopolitics, Racial Mattering, and Queer Affect* by Mel Y. Chen (Durham, NC: Duke University Press, 2012).

"to date stone you" is forever indebted to Leslie Feinberg's classic novel *Stone Butch Blues* (Ann Arbor, MI: Firebrand Books, 1993).

"Quarry: hazards" is indebted to research on the Work Safe page http://worksafevic.clients.squiz.net/pages/safety-and-prevention/ your-industry/quarries/about-the-industry/what-are-the-risks

"things a pebble would say if it could say them" quotes the lines "*hold me – I have a flame on my tongue/ hold me – you are a mouth of water/ hold me – we taste of tangerines/ hold me*" from Rigoberto González's poem "The Border Crosser's Pillowbook" on page 49 of the collection *Unpeopled Eden* (New York: Four Way Books, 2013).

"Quarry: mined" is inspired research on the "Pits and Quarries" page of the website TechnoMine http://technology.infomine.com/reviews/ pitsandquarries/welcome.asp?view=

"that there shall be other fire islands" was inspired by a line from the novel *The Beautiful Room is Empty* by Edmund White (New York: Alfred A. Knopf, 1988):
> *If as a child I'd known my whole long life was going to be painful, I'd never have consented to go on leading it.*

"a spark that starts" was inspired by a quote from *Don't Let Me Be Lonely* by Claudia Rankine (Saint Paul, MN: Graywolf Press, 2004):
> *Such distress moved in with muscle and bone. Its entrance by necessity slowly translated my already grief into a tremendously exhausted hope.*

"Quarry: the pump" is inspired by lines from "Draining and filling in Lac-Chérie could take years, developer says," *Montreal Gazette* September 20, 2013.

"journey fragments" was inspired by *Narrow Road to the Interior* by Matsuo Bashō (Boulder, CO: Shambhala, 2000) and the poem "Notebook Fragments" by Ocean Vuong from the collection *Night Sky with Exit Wounds* (Port Townsend, WA: Copper Canyon Press, 2016).

The lyric quotations come from the songs "Heartwood" and "How can I tell if I'm really in love?" written and performed by S. Ayton (sayton.bandcamp.com). Thank you S. Ayton for your songs and for permission to use these lyrics.

Earlier versions of the following poems have previously appeared in the following publications:

"anthroposcopy" in *Polychrome Ink*

"voyeur" and "the ocean taught me how to cruise" (then entitled "the ocean taught me its smooth talk") in *Contemporary Verse II*

"two people who held each other intensely outside a bar for upwards of twenty minutes" in *The Impressment Gang*

"cal says" on Metatron's *Omega* blog

"february downfall" in *Grain*, along with "waves," "glass," and "signs of dishonesty," appearing there as a three-part poem entitled "glassworks"

"projections" in *Cosmonauts Avenue*

"a ship" in *Vetch*

"flesh of my flesh" in *Matrix*

Thank you to the editors of the above-mentioned publications.

acknowledgements

Endless thanks to my friends for inspiration, for your words, for listening, for existing: Vivian Huang, for your wisdom and saturnal navigation, Jes Dolan, for believing and editing, C. Higgins, for knowing all, and Gisèle. Thank you to the Coven for careful reading and edits (Raena, Laura, Alicia). Charlie J. Meyers, thank you for the use of your perfect painting. To Sina Queyras, Gail Scott, Trish Salah, and Stephanie Bolster for advice, comments, encouragement, and words. To Helen Hajnoczky, Alison Cobra, Melina Cusano, and everyone at University of Calgary Press. Thank you to all the authors previously mentioned for your words, as well.

I remain grateful also to the Conseil des arts et des lettres du Québec for assistance during the completion of this manuscript.

about the author

Tanis Franco's writing has been published in *Room*, *Grain*, *Vetch*, and elsewhere, and anthologized in *Best American Experimental Writing 2018*. They live in Toronto.

Brave & Brilliant Series

SERIES EDITOR:
Aritha van Herk, Professor, English, University of Calgary
ISSN 2371-7238 (Print) ISSN 2371-7246 (Online)

Brave & Brilliant encompasses fiction, poetry, and everything in between and beyond. Bold and lively, each with its own strong and unique voice, Brave & Brilliant books entertain and engage readers with fresh and energetic approaches to storytelling and verse, in print or through innovative digital publication.

No. 1 · **The Book of Sensations**
Sheri-D Wilson

No. 2 · **Throwing the Diamond Hitch**
Emily Ursuliak

No. 3 · **Fail Safe**
Nikki Sheppy

No. 4 · **Quarry**
Tanis Franco